# Where the Pits Were
## Poems from Easington Colliery

## Mary Nightingale Bell

Copyright © Mary Nightingale Bell
All rights reserved.
ISBN: 1479308331
ISBN-13: 978-1479308330

# DEDICATION

To my late husband and dearly loved grandson, Stuart, my family and miners everywhere.

# CONTENTS

Acknowledgements ..................................................................... i
Nightmare .................................................................................. 1
Coal ............................................................................................ 3
Miners ........................................................................................ 4
Pitman Beware .......................................................................... 6
The Spirit of Easington ............................................................. 7
To the Pitmen of Easington ...................................................... 9
Metamorphosis Unseen .......................................................... 11
Idioms ...................................................................................... 12
A Summer Romance ............................................................... 14
The Unwelcome Guest ............................................................ 18
The Tanner Hop ...................................................................... 20
A Tooth for a Tooth ................................................................ 22
The Hippodrome's Epitaph .................................................... 24
In Memoriam East ................................................................... 26
The Elses .................................................................................. 29
Talk of the Devil ...................................................................... 31
Me I Think ............................................................................... 33
Gloves ...................................................................................... 35
A Christmas Present ................................................................ 36
Waiting with Love ................................................................... 37
Pit Head Baths ......................................................................... 39
Coal Dust in my Veins ............................................................ 41
Harvest of the Sea ................................................................... 42
Love Affair ............................................................................... 43
Easington Pit Yard ................................................................... 45
Easington Pit Disaster ............................................................. 47
Easington Pit Disaster 60 years on ......................................... 49
Pitman's Puzzle ....................................................................... 50
Pitmen 1992 ............................................................................. 51
Redundant Miner .................................................................... 52
Nightline .................................................................................. 54
To Pitwomen Sonic Boom ...................................................... 56
Daydream ................................................................................ 57
The Pit Strike ........................................................................... 59
A Sweet Tooth ......................................................................... 63
Leap Year ................................................................................. 66
The Path of Poetry .................................................................. 67

| | |
|---|---|
| Born to Obey | 68 |
| First Love | 69 |
| How to Pray | 70 |
| Life's Little Pleasures | 71 |
| Friendship | 73 |
| St. Cuthbert | 74 |
| Pilgrimage to Holy Island | 76 |
| An Embarrassing Incident | 78 |
| Alone | 80 |
| Big Meeting in the Thirties | 82 |
| Bewitching Night | 84 |
| A Lesson of Life | 86 |
| Antenatal Chat | 87 |
| Derelict House | 89 |
| Easington Colliery Lost | 90 |
| Satisfaction from Changes at a Hospital | 92 |
| Santa Claus and Me | 94 |
| Midnight New Years Eve | 96 |
| A Child in Wartime | 98 |
| Silent Madness | 99 |
| My Moon | 100 |
| The Pit Manager's House | 102 |
| George and Papermoon | 104 |
| I Was a Witness | 105 |
| Miner Not Reinstated | 106 |
| I Hate Women's Lib | 107 |
| On The Way to Church | 108 |
| Passing Through | 110 |
| Tartarus | 112 |
| Mourning | 114 |

# ACKNOWLEDGMENTS

This is a selection of poems written by me over the years. I hope what comes through is my love of the community I grew up in and the miners. I hope you enjoy reading these poems and you will read them over and over again. Thanks to my late husband, Jim and Peter Dickens, great grandson of the famous writer Charles who encouraged me. Peter was Commander of the destroyer Blencathra which my husband served on in the Second World War and many thanks to my children and grandchildren, friends and the miners, the Easington Writers and especially to Terry Dobson who edited this and helped me in lots of ways and the many people who encouraged me

Mary N. Bell.

Mary Nightingale Bell

# NIGHTMARE
by a nurse married to a miner.


We caught the train to London,
Some folk from Scotland were on,
Hearing us say to friends Tarah,
They said you are from where the pits are,

We arrived at the city at ten,
We were eager to see famous Big Ben,
When we asked someone How far,
They said you are from where the pits are.

We spent the weekend there,
Watched the guards change in the square,
When they heard us shout Hurrah,
They said you are from where the pits are.

Every time we stopped and spoke,
Up came the London folk,
We said How are yer there marrah,
They said you are from where the pits are.

They wined and dined us in the strand,
Said miners are the best in the land,
We admire them near and far,
Proudly we said We are from where the pits are.

## Where the Pits Were

We heard a rumour it couldn't be true,
No job for me, no job for you,
The hospital's shut – the pit's gone too,
So we said What are we to do.

We went along to see Mrs. T.,
She looked down at him and at me,
Told us The North East is bare,
You are from where the pits WERE.

**n.b. Mrs. Thatcher was prime minister at the time.**

# COAL

You are black, shiny and round,
What is the cost,
Of getting you out of the ground,
What has been lost,
Bringing you up to the land,
The cost was high,
Stevie's leg and Billy's right hand.
Young men die,
There goes an 'old man'
He's only forty-four,
Stops as he passes,
To get his breath at my door.
Lungs ruined by the gasses,
That men breathe in down the hole.
When you're cosy and warm,
By the fire, burning best coal,
Pray 'keep them from harm'.
Why do they do it,
Why do they descend,
And risk their lives,
Listen to me,
I'll tell you my friend,
For money for their wives,
But go with them and
You'll hear them say
As the mine under the sea,
Coal not dole for me.

## MINERS

Why do I admire you,
What do I see there,
Is it the soft smile on your lips,
Or the shine on your well washed hair.

No it's the something special,
You have been destined to do,
The experience I see in your eyes,
That draws me to you.

In all of your daily lives,
You have known both heaven and hell,
One is the glorious sunlight,
The other, the pit with its strange smell.

Shift after long stinking shift,
I know of your mortal danger,
Death, accidents, limbs lost,
To you they are no stranger.

The courage and protective care,
Of one miner for another,
It is the feeling known to a few,
As though each is the others brother.

Mary Nightingale Bell

Every man depends on the next,
To keep each safe and sound,
There is a special unity,
I sense you have underground.

Whenever I go on a journey,
On land, sea or by air,
I can pick you out of many,
Because of the great man I see there.

Strength, might, grit and guts,
On your face I can see,
The greatest in all the world,
That is what you are to me.

# PITMAN BEWARE

I dominate this place and you revolve around me,
Mesmerised, hypnotised you are drawn to see,
If I am a dream or a constant nightmare,
It is no hallucination. I am there.
Step into my cage, at the ring of a bell,
Plummet through the earth to a special hell,
If I wish I'll do you harm,
I'll break a limb, a leg or an arm,
Respect me or I'll take your life,
Make your child an orphan, a widow your wife,
Breathe in my stench, gasses and dust,
Dig and get coal from my seams if you must,
But pitman beware, you have one life to lose,
And I will take it whenever I choose.

Mary Nightingale Bell

# THE SPIRIT OF EASINGTON

I feel a hand tap me,
On the shoulder,
A voice says hello,
Before I turn around,
I am sure it is someone,
That I know.

The air, sharp and fresh,
From the brisk North Sea,
As is the humour
Of my community.

The view, the backdrop,
Gives me a safe feeling,
The sea, close, unabated,
Without it alongside,
I am completely
Disorientated.

There is a special,
Loyal atmosphere,
I am part of,
I belong here.

## Where the Pits Were

Sea, beach, dene, cliffs,
Are my good fortune,
I am blessed to be living,
Among finest treasures,
And to God I offer,
Grateful thanksgiving.

Easington, my haven,
Place of my birth,
Whose spirit is the people,
The cream of the earth.

Mary Nightingale Bell

# TO THE PITMEN OF EASINGTON

I stood on the shore,
And looked out to sea,
The waves and the foam,
Fascinate me.

What secrets are there,
Down in the deep,
You won't give away,
Determined to keep.

The crabs and the fish,
The rocks and the sand,
These you reveal as you,
Ebb from the land.

Every day different,
Sending foam in the air,
Peaceful or stormy,
You're calling me there.

I looked much deeper,
And then I found,
I was thinking of the men,
Working underground.

My son, my brother,
There out of sight,
My man, my friend,
With no daylight.

I walk down the street,
I look up and see,
The stretch of water,
That beckons me.

## Where the Pits Were

I wondered why,
But now I know,
It is because that you,
Are down below.

Under the sea,
Beneath the sand,
That's where you are,
Not under the land.

Most precious of men,
The finest of all,
The pitmen of Easington,
God bless, I love you all.

Mary Nightingale Bell

# METAMORPHOSIS UNSEEN

Ere the advent of Genesis,
From nature an impressive deed,
Huge and awesome forests,
Grew from an insignificant seed.

Untouched for generations,
Trees died, crashed to the ground,
Sinking slowly 'neath sand and mud,
No trace nor risen mound.

To the dead wood and leaves,
Showing nature skilfully strange,
Rotting vegetable matter
Plus chemicals created a change.

Electric, Gas, Energy,
Drawn from this transformation,
A confusion of diverse uses,
Hewn from a brilliant creation.

This unique miracle of ages past,
With its vital kindling role,
Is a black shining diamond,
Known to us earthly colliers as coal.

# IDIOMS

We went down south, we took the bus,
Folk down there couldn't understand us,
They didn't narr what we tarrked about,
Seemed they didn't narr nowt about owt,
Didn't take hold when we said Tack harrd,
They way they spke you'd have thought they'd of narred,
Hi marra, keep gannin', what fettel,
Cum ower here and we'll hettel,
Ter gan and see the bloody tower,
We'll se yer there at quarter past fower,
They hadn't cum by haff past ite,
We were hungry and went for a bite,
When we asked for a bit of fadge,
It was easier ter gan and cadge
Bread from them we couldn't tarrrk right,
They passed the plate and called it a plite,
They're a very bad speaking clan,
Don't say LUNDUN but LANDAN,
They spread their bread with batter not butter,
Never heard of a hewer or a putter,
What we ate we couldn't tell,
What we wanted we knew darned well,
On our beef we wanted mustard,
They said you mean MASSTAD,
We smothered our apple pie with custard,
On theirs – guess what – CASSTAD.

## Mary Nightingale Bell

After we said we were gannin yem,
They made sure we understood them,
Cos yer narr what they went and sayed,
They wished we'd a gone and stayed,
Cos they loved our pitmatic twang,
Our northern accent and bits of slang.
They saw us on the bass not the bus,
On parting they said this to us,
Even though we didn't narr out,
That yae were gannin on about,
We pray that you will also speak so,
And never let your accent go.

## A SUMMER ROMANCE

I stood at the bus stop,
Early one morning,
A wonderful thing happened,
With no warning,
Here was a young man,
Slim-handsome-tall,
Waiting beside me,
Plump-so-so and small,
Where had he come from,
This handsome young knight,
Standing aside and aloof,
I fancy him alright.

All day long,
With mind in the air,
I thought of him,
Who had been standing there,
Day after day,
Regular as can be,
He was at the bus stop,
Tormenting me.
Every day the bus came,
Not a minute late,
No time for him,
To ask for a date.

One day he spoke,
I am you know really,
A very shy bloke,
Will you meet me tonight,
At half past eight?
Would I? Yes- yes,
I couldn't wait.
Where do you live?
It fair made my day,

Mary Nightingale Bell

To hear that he,
Lived across the way,
From me.
And I vowed to myself,
That every night,
I would look across,
To see his light.

We met and then,
We took a walk,
I found out,
He couldn't half talk,
He was one of those-,
Educated man.
He took me home,
I went in and then,
In the middle
Of that hot, sleepless night,
Looked out of the window,
To see his light,
Shining through the blind,
Pulled discreetly down,
His shadow I could see,
Jumping round and round,
An arm thrown out,
He jumped off the bed,
Bounced up again,
I could just see his head.

Trust me, I thought,
To fancy somebody queer,
He had no business,
To come and live near,
To tantalise me,
With blue eyes and tan,

## Where the Pits Were

If he wasn't,
A real macho man.
The very next day,
I missed the bus,
I didn't really,
Want to make a fuss,
About what I'd seen,
That peculiar sight,
Of him silhouetted,
In the bright lamplight.
He looked normal,
He seemed alright,
I'd watch again,
Another night,
Same thing again,
Arms swinging round,
The he was, stamping,
On the ground,
An Indian war dance?
I pondered on that,
I didn't think that they,
Danced on the mat,

We met again,
His arm in a sling,
How did it happen?
He'd had a fling,
I knew that,
I'd watched each night,
As he cavorted,
Neath the electric light,
What's coming next?
'I fell off the bed,
I hurt my arm,
And bruised my head,

Mary Nightingale Bell

The worst of the summer,
I can't rest at night,
Before I go to sleep,
I kill –
Every moth in sight'.

# THE UNWELCOME GUEST

Come to my house,
Call on me,
You can be sure,
Of a cup of tea.

A welcome here
For those who call,
The doors are open,
To one and all.

Come any day,
There's sure to be,
A slice of cake,
With hot coffee.

Bring a friend,
Your sister too,
Stay for a meal,
I'll entertain you.

Come for breakfast,
Stay to tea,
Any excuse,
I'll give a party.

I thought that I,
Loved one and all,
Till someone else,
Came to call.

He ate my cake,
He ate my cheese,
He was very, very,
Easy to please.

He ate the bread,
And after that,
He ate a bit,
Of Jim's old hat.

He brought his wife,
She frightened me,
I didn't want her,
To stay to tea.

Something happened,
They'd have to go,
I hadn't the guts,
To tell them so.

What to do,
I'd had my fill,
Of this couple,
Kill- Kill- Kill.

What a thought,
To come to my head,
Here am I wishing,
This guest was dead.

I didn't think,
Murder would come,
Into my heart,
And in my home.

What about weapon,
Hammer or spade,
Or the kitchen knife,
With the sharpest blade.

## Mary Nightingale Bell

What to use,
For this wicked deed,
I couldn't stand,
To see them bleed.

Get out – go- go,
Is what I said,
When they began,
To share my bed.

They didn't speak,
Just looked at me,
Then they brought,
Their family.

So off I went,
I moved away,
I couldn't murder,
I'm sorry to say.

I've always been,
Placid and kind,
What happened you ask,
To change my mind,

Who was it-,
Who called at my house,
His name---?
Mr. Mouse.

# THE TANNER HOP

The scene is set, no tables,
Chairs lined against the wall,
The band strikes up the quickstep,
In everyman's dance hall.

Across the crowded room,
The brave lads stride,
To ask a girl to dance,
So proper and dignified.

He takes her in his arms,
Leads her, quick, quick, slow,
Stepping out in harmony,
Round and round they go.

The saxophone, the trumpet,
The piano and big bass,
The drummer and musicians,
Add enchantment to the pace.

Now for some old fashioned,
Barn dance, sequence, valeeta,
Boston two step, St. Bernard's,
Movement, tempo and metre.

In the ladies excuse me,
I always lose my partner,
Fuming I sit it out,
Too proud to return the 'favour'.

Modern waltz and tango,
Foxtrot to many tunes,
Thoughts of romance inspired,
By the words the singer croons.

Mary Nightingale Bell

Sixpence paid at the door,
No alcohol allowed,
Ensured a euphoric night,
With a lively, sparkling crowd.

Save the last dance for me,
Meant, can I take you home,
A kiss goodnight on the doorstep.
And a date at the Hippodrome.

# A TOOTH FOR A TOOTH

I happened by chance,
To look from my window,
What act did I see,
Going on down below,
A thug or a vandal,
Lifted his big foot,
Kicked in my window,
With his Doc Martens boot.

There in my brain,
Though we hadn't met,
This young thugs face
I couldn't forget,
Taken to court,
Punishment was none,
He said he was just -,
Having a bit of fun.

One day guess what,
An answer to my prayer,
This young person,
Was sitting in my chair,
Open wide, I said,
What have we got here,
One or two to be filled,
You're shaking with fear.

Close your eyes then,
A whiff of the mask,
I will soon finish,
My pleasing gory task.
I believe lots of things,
Like telling the truth,
An eye for an eye,
And a tooth for a tooth.

## Mary Nightingale Bell

My prayers are answered,
He came just in time,
I would make the punishment,
Fit the crime.
What had he done ?
Given my window a clout,
While he is well under,
I'll take all his teeth out.

I pulled all his teeth,
Dropped them into his lap,
We both - now - had -,
A- great - big - gap,
Mine in the wall -,
His - in the gob -,
I got my own back,
Doing this bloody job.

He woke and he screamed,
What's this you have done,
It's all right, I'm just a dentist,
Having a bit of fun.

## THE HIPPODROME'S EPITAPH

They're pulling the Hippodrome down,
And what tales the bricks could tell,
Of courting, dating and engagements,
And a few broken hearts as well.

Now it's to be a memory,
To be stored here in my brain,
I'm beginning to like getting old,
So that I can remember again.

Rain, wind, sun or snow,
You'd see me set out from home,
Three nights a week to see,
The film on at the Hippodrome.

What pictures are you going to tonight,
Was a phrase you heard on the street,
I'll see you outside the Hippodrome,
Friends and lovers would arrange to meet.

A queue to book your seat,
Was a regular weekend scene,
To make sure you didn't miss,
The film on the silver screen.

Look who's coming in with who,
Don't they make a handsome pair,
See who that good lookers with,
Whatever does he see in her.

When the picture began to reel,
Every one was quiet and still,
Any person who spoke out of turn,
George gave a look fit to kill.

Mary Nightingale Bell

For a couple of hours peace,
If you left the kids at home,
For one and six or less,
You could relax in the Hippodrome.

I'm glad I was born when I was,
Or I would never have known,
That where houses will be in the future,
Once stood our beloved Hippodrome.

# IN MEMORIAM EAST

A hundred colliery houses,
With a thousand tales to tell,
Walking the streets of Easington,
 I heard the tolling of a funeral bell.

There is no mourning party,
No one to shed a tear,
These sombre bells are pealing,
For the memories buried here.

I stopped at the shell of a house,
And looked at the windows so bare.
Did I glimpse a movement,
Or is it ghosts I see everywhere.

Now wedding bells are ringing,
I can feel the happiness,
As the lovely bride appears,
In her shining white satin dress

The midwife's at number ten,
The neighbours all know why,
So they stand at their gates waiting,
To hear a baby's first cry.

Whenever there was an illness,
Someone always knew a cure,
A bereavement in the family,
Help would soon be at your door.

Each knew what went on,
In one house and another,
Not prying, nosey or meddling,
They all cared about each other.

Mary Nightingale Bell

An accident at the pit,
Husband, father or son,
All East would volunteer,
To help the unlucky one.

A difference in a back street,
Wasn't seen as a fight on the news,
An argument was settled,
By listening to the others views.

As I walk through the streets,
I puzzle and ponder,
What made the people special,
What was the wonder.

I look towards the north,
I see the pulley wheels-that's it,
In every house there lived a man,
Who worked at Easington pit.

Now the bells ring happily,
A thought comes to my head,
The memories might be buried,
But they'll never be lost or dead.

Did I see a broken window?
Litter, a mouse or a rat,
No. as I walked the streets,
I didn't notice any of that

## Where the Pits Were

Vandalism, graffiti, rubbish,
Dilapidation was all there,
But the feel of the past can never be seen,
Love, kindness, goodness and care.

The past is past,
Back to the future,
Goodbye East,
Goodbye yesteryear

Mary Nightingale Bell

# THE ELSES

THE ELSES, you've heard of them,
EVERBODY, NOBODY and SOMEBODY,
To everyone's family, they are,
Some kind of mystic parody.

EVERBODY ELSE watches the late movie,
Has chips every single day,
Lies in bed till noon – if they want,
And always get their own way.

EVERBODY ELSE is going to Disneyland,
Then to Africa to do some exploring,
EVERYBODY ELSES dad hires a D.V.D.,
When the computer becomes boring.

EVERYBODY ELSE gets more pocket money,
EVERYBODY ELSE stays out late,
Then there is NOBODY ELSE,
He certainly pulls his weight.

NOBODY ELSE does the washing up,
Goes to bed early or keeps their room clean,
Drinks milk or weeds the garden,
NOBODY ELSE'S dad is so mean.

What about SOMEBODY ELSE,
Who broke the handle off the door,
Left the bathroom tap running,
Until it flooded the floor.

SOMEBODY ELSE, always unseen,
Lost the remote control of the T.V.,
Left the top off the pop bottle,
And mislaid the front door key.

After every weekend,
And at the end of each holiday,
You, me and EVERYBODY ELSES parents,
All shout Hip, Hip Hooray.
Still wondering about the ELSES,
Who on earth are they.

Mary Nightingale Bell

# TALK OF THE DEVIL

I met the devil- Old Nick,
On Easington pit site,
Sitting in the old pit cage,
Gave me a heck of a fright.

Me granda talked of Old Nick,
Said he knew him well,
Told him nee heaven for us,
We'd all gan ter hell.

Me granda always sayed,
Nee different from the pit,
I'll feel at home in hell,
Aam reet used to it.

Nick sucked on his pipe,
Blew out a lot of smoke,
Smelled of sulphur and brimstone.
And – then – he – spoke.

Aah narred the granda,
Met him down the pit,
He didn't gan soft in the head,
Was just crackin' on a bit.

Davey, arr reet lad,
Aa've been waitin' for thou,
Thee granda was a rotter,
Aa telt him what aah was ganna do.

## Where the Pits Were

Aam ganna tack all of yer,
Includin' thine and thee,
No heaven for you lot,
Yer all comin' down ter me.

Aam the devil see-,
His eyes were glowing red,
Aa winnet be satisfied,
Till all you lot is dead.

Aa ran from the pit cage,
The blue sky went all black,
A lotta ghosts walk ower there,
Aa've – not – been – back.

Mary Nightingale Bell

# ME I THINK

What did I come in this room for?
Sugar for my tea?
I haven't made any and,
I don't take sugar, silly me.
Where on earth did I put it?
Now let me see ---,
In the cupboard or knife drawer,
What on earth
Am I looking for?
I'll remember it sometime,
Find it one day,
When I look for another thing,
Then I won't want it anyway.

That good looking bloke,
You know the one,
You knew him quite well,
Was his name Joe, George or John?
He ran away with somebody's wife,
Her name I can't recall,
Caused quite a scandal,
She was blonde, skinny and small.
I can't quite remember,
But I'll tell you what,
I'll ring you at 2.30 in the morning,
With all the info I've got.
It will come in a flash,
A burst of brilliant insight,
My mind works fast overtime,
In the middle of the night.

## Where the Pits Were

There goes the phone,
Do you want a new kitchen?
No, I'd like a chat,
Tell you what I really want,
A new, pink, feathery hat,
Oh! She's put the phone down,
Now – I wonder why?
She thinks I'm barmy,
But me, I'm still quite fly,
Got rid of her pretty quickly,
With a little, white lie.

# GLOVES

A drawer full of odd socks,
Not in my house,
A drawer full of odd gloves,
That's what I've got,
Woolly ones, posh leather,
Lace and cotton too.

All dressed up with
Glove on each hand,
Shop and spend till I drop,
It's happened again,
One hand is bare,
Why can't I lose a pair?

I have to keep the one,
In case I find the other,
Gloves from a lifetime,
Are in my drawer,
All odd and varied,
Nothing to make a pair.

Brainwave solution,
Go barehanded or –
I could start a fashion,
Wearing odd gloves,
Sift through a hundred,
No luck there,
All left handed!!
Buy another pair.

# A CHRISTMAS PRESENT

A Christmas gift, we all get one,
Samuel Pepys, Adrian Mole and me,
It's taken me till now to read it,
The title? The Yearly Diary.

It is full of utter trivia,
And a lot of gobbledy gook,
You want to know the time in China,
I'll just look it up in this book.

It tells the day of every saint,
Changes a gallon to a litre,
Did you know in the U.S.
A helicopter's an eggbeater?

Lighting up times in every town,
How many miles to India,
I can guarantee this book,
Is an instant cure for insomnia.

Its got a lot of handy maps,
Of London Underground,
A wine vintage chart with symbols,
And how many grains in a pound.

My head is over flowing,
With all its facts and data,
World temperature guides,
And how many miles to the equator.

Best of all is the space,
For writing all I should do,
Trouble is that part is empty,
In March! I'm still busy reading it through.

Mary Nightingale Bell

# WAITING WITH LOVE

There's been an accident at the pit,
I'm absolutely sure of it,
He should have been here ten minutes ago,
Something's happened, bet I'll be the last to know,
Please God let him be alright,
And I'll say my prayers every night.
He should have been here at quarter to one,
That's when I had his dinner all done,
Another hour has gone by,
If he comes home now it'll be a fry.
Please God keep him safe for me,
And I'll be good as good can be,
No nagging him to wipe his feet,
When he comes in from the dirty street,
I'll make sure his life's all honey,
Not even tell him how to spend his pocket money.
Please God don't let him have a lame,
And every Sunday I'll make church my aim.
He hasn't come yet, my eyes fill with tears,
I think it's happened, the worst of my fears,
I'll tell him I love him every day,
And never again want my own way,
God send him home without delay,
And I'll come to church and never stray.
Should I phone the pit or wait?
One last time I'll go to the gate.
Here he's coming- he's safe and sound,
And me thinking he was hurt underground,
There he is safe, and me worried to death,
He's hurrying and laughing and quite out of breath,

## Where the Pits Were

All right, where've you been, what's that?
You've seen Geordie and had a chat,
About the colour and rust on his leeks,
I'll not speak to you for weeks and weeks,
Here you are, safe, and me white with fright,
You'll make your own dinner tomorrow night.
Sorry Lord, I can't come to church just yet,
But I'll think of an excuse by Sunday, don't fret.

Mary Nightingale Bell

# PIT HEAD BATHS

From the dark pit below,
The cage rushes to the top,
It reaches the surface
Jolts to a sudden stop.

Figures streams out,
All orange and black,
White helmets on heads,
All looking alike.

They head for the baths,
Longing for a shower,
To wash away the stench,
They worked in down there.

Some sponge another's back,
With a laugh and a joke,
While others satisfy the need,
Of a long awaited smoke.

Washing and scrubbing,
What a strange sight,
These coal black pitmen,
All wash white.

They walk from the baths,
Different from the cage,
They are changed like characters,
Playing parts on the stage.

## Where the Pits Were

The stink of the pit,
That has gone too,
They smell of aftershave, deodorant,
And my favourite shampoo.

In the theatre of life,
Pitmen act a strange role,
To supply England with fuel,
They tunnel like a mole.

These men I admire,
I state with great zest,
Are the most bewitching, cleanest,
As well as the best

Mary Nightingale Bell

# COAL DUST IN MY VEINS

Pits, miners, coal,
Companions of my life,
Proud pitman's daughter,
Loyal colliers wife,
Gallower, kist, pit prop,
Hewer, stoneman, putter,
Were the very first words,
I was heard to utter,
Deputy grandad,
Easington born and bred,
Poems and stories of coal,
stockpiled in my head,
In hundreds of years time,
when they dig up my remains,
Descendants will find I have
Coal dust in my veins.

# HARVEST OF THE SEA

You ebb and flow to the land and away,
Bringing riches to the shore day after day,
Round all of the coast except the North East band,
You wash gold to the shore and call it sand.
Reap what you sew, a well known proverb,
What is our harvest, what do we deserve,
Look from the cliffs at what we have done,
Planted coal in the sea and reaped what we've sewn.
We threw out our stone and unwanted slack,
Never dreaming the sea would wash it all back.
Grey horses dance and stir up the foam,
Tiding coal to the shore it went from.
Is dirty black sand our harvest of the sea?
Not in my sight, for coal is gold to me.

Mary Nightingale Bell

# LOVE AFFAIR

I had this dream see,
Turned to a night mare,
I went to see you,
You weren't there.

I stood at the place,
Where we met often,
The field was empty,
Dust and bracken,

You broke my heart,
Again and again,
Killing and hurting,
Like a wild hurricane.

It was a mad love affair,
Between you and me,
Since you've gone,
I'm not sorry I'm free.

You were always there,
I'd always had you,
Love turned to hate,
At the things you'd do.

Now you've gone,
In my heart I'm glad,
I sigh for the future,
Hope it's not too bad.

## Where the Pits Were

I treasure your memory,
That's all far behind,
Redundant, renewed,
I have peace of mind.

This affair of mine,
Deep, dark, secret,
Ended gone for good,
Was with THE PIT.

Mary Nightingale Bell

# EASINGTON PIT YARD

Surrounded by high walls,
Forbidding facade,
'Men only' territory,
Is Easington pit yard.

Invading male domain,
My heart went pit a pat,
I entered the pit yard,
And donned safety hat.

I expected to see,
Coal handpicked and then,
It washed and sorted,
By scores of men.

No picks and shovels,
Not even a broom,
As Alan led me,
To the computer room.

Information flow,
Maths and simulation,
Processing, programming,
Digits of combination.

Visual display,
Underground on the screen,
Water pumps working,
Plus a coal cutting machine.

Controls, rotations,
Quality and tonnage,
Beyond comprehension,
This computer language.

## Where the Pits Were

Belt, cage and washer,
Grader robot,
Operated by one man,
Finger on a dot.

The pit computers,
Are a mystery to me,
Not to be outdone,
By visual display unit T.V.

Electronic systems
Or clever masculinity,
I've enrolled to study,
For a university degree.

Mary Nightingale Bell

# EASINGTON PIT DISASTER

Head bowed at the foot of the mass grave,
Atmosphere serene and quiet,
My mind zoomed instantly back to the past,
Imagination running riot.

May twenty ninth nineteen fifty-one,
Can you hear the clash of a gate,
As an unsuspecting pit lad checks,
He has his water bottle and bait.

He glances back at his home,
Unaware of what lies ahead,
Not knowing the echoing sound,
Is his swansong, unsung, unread.

Pit baths, change clothes, catch cage,
Travel rocky underground hills,
Eighty one ill-fated coal getters,
Walk to death in the North Pit duck Bills.

The explosion rocked the pit,
Black killer dust, white-hot hell,
To add to the anguish of Easington,
Two rescuers perished as well.

Jim, Jack, Tom, Bill Joe,
Jesse, Peter, Bert and john,
George, Mattie, Steve, Fred, Hughie,
A few of the names that we mourn.

## Where the Pits Were

Names written on the memorial,
On the hill overlooking the sea,
Ensuring the disaster of Easington,
Is forever preserved in history.

Accountants are able to reckon,
Politicians fight to control,
Argue prices, rates and profits,
Easington knows the cost of coal.

Mary Nightingale Bell

# EASINGTON PIT DISASTER 60 YEARS ON

Sixty years on,
In Easington,
At the foot of the mass grave,
I stand and mourn.

The pit where 83 died
Is shut, filled in,
Silent, a field
Where I walk.

Voices echo in my head,
The tramp of pit boots,
The clang of the trucks,
The smell of the pit.

Disaster 1951,
Generations pass the story on,
Pit wheel, pit site, pit cage,
Memorial Avenue, Memorial Garden,

Monuments and records left,
For, descendants to know,
And never forget,
Men lived and died
For coal.
In Easington,
In 1951.

## PITMAN'S PUZZLE

The AUTHOR writes a story,
Published as a book,
The HAIRDRESSER creates a style,
And gives a client a new look,
The GARDENER plants a seed,
Which grow to beautiful flowers,
The CLAIRVOYANT tells the future,
With their strange, mystic powers,
The CARWORKER looks with pride,
On the car he has made,
BUILDERS admire, the houses,
That are products of their trade,
A PAINTER'S work is enjoyed,
On canvas or ceiling,
A DOCTOR sees a patient,
Whose illness is healing.
I come in from the pit,
Can this sight be true?
The product of my work,
SMOKE- vanishing up the flue

Mary Nightingale Bell

# PITMEN 1992

Never to be forgotten,
13th October 1992,
Executor Heseltine spoke,
England I've bad news for you.

Easington, your pit's shut from now,
And you are not on your own,
President of the Board of Trade,
I plan to shut thirty one.

In times of trouble and war,
 Who rallies to the crown,
Loyal pitmen of England
Above and below the ground.

Betrayed by governing Tories,
Smarting and cruelly abandoned,
Famed for united communities,
Pitmen are to be a legend.

Never to be forgotten,
Through my stories and poetry,
I will wrote and record,
Our standards were no mystery,
We were people living and warm,
Who made mining history.

# REDUNDANT MINER

He stands, doffs cap as though there is a death,
Panting, resting, lungs dust clogged, to get his breath,
Reflects in his mind's eye as he looks up to the sky,
The clouds like bonny pit banners flying high,
Draped in black where there had been a man killed,
The banners are redundant, the pit wheels forever stilled.

A hyper modern supermarket is planned,
For the space where the pulley wheels used to stand,
Pit yards lawned over are a factory site,
Where workers will never again leave daylight,
Never step into the cage, hear the bell,
Then drop underground to a coal black hell.

Breathless and heart beating like a drum, he stops for a bit,
A man who was never alone in the pit,
Remembering the special feel one had for another,
In the stinking hole, as though each was the others' brother,
Now he is alone in his redundancy,
Gone is his caring pit community.

The wives, they aren't there any more,
He remembered how the women would be standing at the door,
Of a man late home from the mine,
Alone he stands as he remembers the time,
When his banner wasn't draped in black,
How he'd dance and sing and stop for a bit crack.

Now the fading pit banners in his minds eye,
Are draped in black, he saw each pit die,
Thornley, the Knack, Wingate, Blackhall, Horden,
South Hetton, Eppleton, Haswell and Shotton,
Colliery houses are all gone,
With work and free coal from this void region.

No joy in racing pigeons or dogs these days,
No young 'uns' around to teach his wily old ways,
Hear grating in the back street, the rattle of the craig,
As it calls the lifeless pits from their grave,
Come there's a union meeting in the Welfare Hall,
See the dead pitmen heed the craig's summoning call.

Gallowers, they must enjoy running free,
Big Tom, Bonny Prince and Black Beauty,
The last of their kind to be bred,
He is the last of his and will soon be dead,
Like this once thriving pit community,
He'll be part of North East history.

But the miner will never be forgotten,
For descendants will read the words I have written,
In my stories and poems and local rhymes,
I have recorded how he lived, loved and laughed in these times.

# NIGHTLINE

Watching from my window,
I am awed by the sight,
The railway bridge looks sculpted,
A phantom shape in the night.

The stars shine like diamonds,
In the midnight blue sky,
The whole world is sleeping,
Except the full moon and I.

From the darkness of the North,
An express speeds down the line,
Passing the empty trucks,
Racing busily to the mine.

The night train is travelling,
Through York and Peterborough,
The passengers sleeping,
Won't wake till tomorrow.

For holidays and pleasure,
People journey on the train,
Rushing to the airport,
To catch the sunshine plane.

The full moon and I,
Are the only ones to know,
The coal trucks are travelling,
To the darkness below.

Mary Nightingale Bell

Not awake on my own,
As I watch the railway line,
The whole world isn't sleeping,
Men are digging down the mine.

Coal getters of the night,
We have an affinity,
All the world is sleeping,
Except the full moon, you and me.

# TO PITWOMEN SONIC BOOM

At the beginning of November,
In nineteen ninety eight,
Woman took a step back,
To a very early date.

A rumbling was heard,
The earth moved in waves,
Nineteenth century women,
Turned over in their graves.

Modern women's lib.,
Was the cause of it,
They had fought and won,
The right to work down the pit.

Silly women's lib.,
Men let you win that fight,
Detail dirty jobs to them,
Then you'll have it right.

Females of last century,
Had the right idea,
Preaching we're of most import,
And males the inferior.

Dear ancestral sisters,
Rest at peace in death,
Some of us have learned,
The lessons that you left.

Use your feminine guile,
Act intelligent or dumb,
Do not accept equality,
Keep men well under your thumb.

Mary Nightingale Bell

# DAYDREAM

Browsing casually,
Strolling round the great hall,
I was drawn to this picture,
Hanging on the wall.

It was an old fireplace,
Looked neglected to me,
From an old colliery house,
Dated nineteen hundred and thirty,

Paper, sticks and coal,
In front of my eyes,
There in the empty grate,
Match struck, then a surprise

Orange and red flames,
Pictures in the fire,
Palm trees, a wheel, a dog,
Awed I had to stay and admire,

A wisp of smoke,
Settled in the wood chair,
Mesmerised, entranced,
I continued to stare.

A woman was sitting,
Rocking to and fro,
A babe in her arms,
A delightful duo.

The picture was bright,
Full of love and life,
I knew this woman,
Was a pitman's wife.

## Where the Pits Were

A pie in the oven
Pan on the hob,
I spoke to the woman,
Couldn't hold back a sob.

The picture was gone,
Quick as a flash,
Did I have an insight,
Who lived there in the past

Mary Nightingale Bell

# THE PIT STRIKE

In nineteen eighty four,
On a chill march day,
We are on strike,
I heard the pitmen say.

My heart skipped a beat,
I thought of their wives,
Did they realise the changes,
This would bring to their lives.

No money in your purse,
A pantry that is bare,
No coal to keep you warm,
As you freeze in the cold north air.

It won't be for long,
We'll all come out,
We'll show the N.C.B.
Was the unions' shout.

With plenty of foreign coal,
And no electricity cut,
Did any, but us care,
That the pit was shut.

Watching you search for fuel,
And worrying about bread,
The reason for the strike,
Went from my head.

I never thought that,
My heart could go on aching
For one whole year,
Without its breaking.

## Where the Pits Were

At the beginning,
Your eyes were bright and clear,
As the months went by,
They were filled with fear.

Not for yourselves,
For you are the bravest of men,
But the suffering and worry,
You had brought to your kin.

I went to the town,
Saw you with your bucket,
You looked so downcast,
But you smiled as you shook it.

Calling you for begging,
The woman who passed by,
Said get to work you lazy men,
You are just work shy.

My eyes filled with tears,
As I heard this woman shout,
She did not know what
The strike was about.

I knew what you wanted,
Work for life,
Prosperity forever,
For your family and wife.

There were many others,
And I was one my friend,
Who admired your guts,
And backed you to the end.

Mary Nightingale Bell

Every day of the week,
In the busy soup kitchen,
Cooking meals and serving,
Slaved the women of Easington.

When the winter winds blew,
Station dene became bare,
Men chopped trees for their fires,
They'd grow again next year.

Christmas day came,
And then it went,
No giving or rejoicing,
It was more like Lent,

I saw you go to the pit,
Look up in despair,
At Easington pulley wheels,
So still in the air.

Your thoughts in your eyes,
Am I doing right,
Then turning back home,
To another sleepless night.

Another March day came,
A year has gone past,
The pit strike is over,
At long last.

I'll always remember,
As long as I am alive,
The end of the strike,
In nineteen eighty five.

## Where the Pits Were

I heard the coal trucks,
Clang on the line,
Saw the pulley wheels turn,
To take the men down the mine.

Following the banner,
Your eyes showed the pain,
As forced back to the pit,
You marched down Seaside Lane.

Look the world in the face,
Don't hang your head down,
For I will tell,
Of the strength of Easington.

Mary Nightingale Bell

# A SWEET TOOTH

I'll take a stroll,
Through this new store,
Goodness me there's things,
I've never seen before.

An assortment of gadgets,
In the D.I.Y. section,
Clothes, electrics, toys,
What a diverse selection.

I marvelled at the amount,
Of goods on display,
I didn't plan to spend,
Any money today.

What's in that corner,
Pick'n Mix – take a bag,
Creams, toffee, fudge,
My feet went zig zag.

I have this sweet tooth,
It rules my mind,
I love confectionary,
Of every kind.

Take a bag,
Open it wide,
Pop two or three of each,
Assortment inside.

Five minutes later,
It's such a drag,
I still can't open,
That darned plastic bag.

## Where the Pits Were

A little child,
Licks finger and thumb,
The bag just opens,
I feel so dumb.

A lively young man,
Fingers nipped at the top,
Opens up the bag,
With a brisk pop.

A sweet old lady,
Rubs it 'twixt her palms,
Bag opens wide,
With no qualms.

Try all these ways,
Don't get harassed,
Ask for help,
I'm too embarrassed.

I have learned,
How to get thin,
Use plastic bags,
To put goodies in.

Looking at me,
Seems it's a lie,
It didn't work,
And this is why.

Mary Nightingale Bell

I buy sweets,
Ready boxed,
That man made plastic,
I out foxed.

The plastic bag,
I am the proof,
Cannot outwit,
A genuine sweet tooth.

# LEAP YEAR

Girls get ready for this is your year,
You can propose, so get ready,
Ask for his hand in marriage,
Even if he's another's steady.

If he refuses tradition says,
You can claim a pair of gloves,
But does that compensate if,
You aren't the one he loves.

If Feb. 29$^{th}$ is your birth date,
You'll get the key of the door,
When you reach the ripe old age,
Of four score years and four.

Julius Caesar invented a calendar,
In the year 46 B.C.
365 days, one over every four years,
He created a problem for me.

I am paid by the month,
So my gripe is this you see,
Every leap year, one in four,
I work a day extra for free.

Mary Nightingale Bell

# THE PATH OF POETRY

The path of poetry
Free verse, meter or rhyme,
Future, present, past,
Choose the place or the time.

It leads you to imagine,
Think, laugh, cry,
Use words so descriptive,
The reader will sigh.

Walk along a country lane,
Be a flower, tree or a plant,
Insects, animals, birds,
Spark off a verse or a chant.

A building, sea, sky or man,
A world of inspiration,
The path of poetry has many roads,
Pleasure, anticipation.

You are possessed to write a poem,
Don't want to ever finish,
Words and thoughts in your mind,
You meditate and cherish.

Satisfied you cannot do better,
The next path is bold and exciting,
To share with others by reading,
The pleasure you've had in writing.

Poetry leads you to friendships,
People you would never have known,
If you walk the path of poetry,
You will not walk alone.

# BORN TO OBEY

Standard procedures,
Rules and regulations,
Mandates, laws and doctrines,
Guidelines and legislations,
Set by unions and government of the day,
A pitman is expected,
To conform and obey.

Birth to be registered,
Name on doctor's panel,
School for education,
To tread life's bizarre channel.
At eighteen he can drink,
Smoke and work before this,
Vote and fight for his country,
Enjoy wedded bliss.

Rent, rates and taxes,
Nothing is free,
A licence must be had
For radio, car and T.V.,
At work, down the pit,
Rules to be obeyed,
Transgressions and accounts,
Someday must be paid.

Pitman, poet, everyman,
All the world and his wife,
The dull and the brilliant,
Born into this life,
Live by a rule book,
Brainwashed they have a say,
By decree every man and woman,
Must conform and obey.

# FIRST LOVE

I was so
Broken hearted,
He cast aside,
Unworldly me,
With my dimply
Knees, chin and cheeks,
We parted.
He told me,
He sought,
Fast travel
On wheels.

Will he
Come back,
To me?
'Twas on his birthday,
That he left,
He returned,
Offered to share,
His new love
One of his pair,
Of roller skates
With me.

My first love,
He was four and a day,
I was three,
Shrewdly,
I agreed.

# HOW TO PRAY

You want to talk to God,
And you can't find the words to say,
You want to feel near to God,
And you don't know what to say.

Sit quietly in a room,
Empty your mind of earthly care,
Turn your thoughts to God,
And you will feel he is there.

In your head write a letter,
Dear God, Are you there,
Because I have a few words
I'd like to say to You in prayer.

Thank Him for your good days,
Tell Him if you are troubled,
After praying to God you will feel,
Your blessings are doubled.

When you've said Amen,
And you've finished your prayer,
Your troubles won't seem so bad,
Although they'll still be there.

But God will advise you,
Guide you on the right way,
He'll be at your side,
A staunch true friend day after day.

His rod and His staff,
His comfort, support and stay,
With these you will be blessed,
If you have FAITH and PRAY.

Mary Nightingale Bell

# LIFE'S LITTLE PLEASURES

A dew covered cobweb glistening in the sunlight.
Toasting bread on a coal fire on a wet afternoon.
The smell of bacon cooking.
Finding letters on your doormat and none of them a bill.
Breakfast in bed.
Completing a crossword.
Comfort eating with a like-minded friend.
Bumping into an old friend you haven't seen for years.
The colours of autumn.
Receiving flowers on your birthday.
Receiving flowers for no reason at all.
Splashing through puddles in your welly boots.
A long slow stroll in the country.
Watching newborn foals take their first steps.
The day your puppy is finally house trained.
Waking up and thinking you have to go to work and remembering it's Saturday
Shopping with your best friend.
Browsing in junk shops.
Managing to open a milk carton without spilling it.
Getting your fried egg out of the pan without breaking the yolk.
Being told by the dentist you don't need a filling.
Being offered a job you really want.
Being offered a job you don't want.
Bees buzzing on a summer day.
Cooking the first homegrown vegetables of the year.
The smells of honey suckle.
Warm rain in the middle of a dry summer.
Finding money in the pocket of an old coat
Finding money down the back of an old sofa.
The feel of velvet.
The smell of baking bread.

## Where the Pits Were

Watching a school nativity play.
The first time the baby sleeps through the night.
Walking in the rain.
Listening to your favourite music.
Receiving a valentine card and really not know whose sent it.
Laughing till it hurts
Being given a hug.
Singing along to a brass band very loudly and out of tune.
Listening to a storm raging when you are cosy and warm inside
Losing weight when you haven't been trying.
A spectacular sunset.
Helping someone with research
Helping someone
Four hours in a bookshop.
Writing a poem.
Writing a book.
Chocolate
Having your first book published.
Still frosty mornings.
Finding the remote control.

# FRIENDSHIP

A Friend –
Can be someone you have known all your life.
Can be someone you have just met.
Is someone who always has the time to listen to you.
Is someone who will do something e.g. a favour for you anytime.
Is someone who never says 'you owe me one'.
Can be of any age group not just yours.
Is someone if you have not seen him or her for years is still your friend.
Does not interfere with your life.
Is always there even if they are miles away.
Time does not matter between friends.
You don't have to live in each other's pockets.
If you have a friend like this you have a true friend.
If you are like this you are a true friend.

## ST. CUTHBERT

Walking through Durham Cathedral,
I was drawn to the great High Altar,
To show my respect and admiration,
Of St, Cuthbert who was buried there.

I had a divine experience,
St. Cuthbert touched my hand,
As I bowed in deepest reverence,
He said follow me my friend.

I helped him tend his sheep,
He taught me of animals and flowers,
Took me back to roam the centuries,
And told me of God's wondrous powers.

I watched with him the silver flame,
Lead St. Aidan's spirit to earth,
The sign was like the Eastern Star,
That told of our Saviour's birth.

It inspired our beloved Cuthbert,
To devote his life to the Lord above,
He entered the monastery at Melrose,
And taught our ancestors, God's love.

He touched my cheek and told me,
How he was moved to tears of emotion,
When he was praising and honouring God,
And swearing eternal devotion.

Cuthbert then sought solitude,
With simplicity and love and meditation
Faith, belief, prayer and trust,
He became our Holy Inspiration.

Mary Nightingale Bell

A light flashing from his exile,
Told that he'd left and gone on,
To sit at God's right hand,
And was with his brother Aidan.

Four centuries later the monks,
After travelling from village to town,
Brought the earthly remains of Cuthbert,
To where I honour, revere and kneel down.

On May the first, nineteen forty four,
Luftwaffe planes on a raid,
Planned to bomb Durham cathedral,
And blast St. Cuthbert from his grave.

As the aircraft flew overhead,
The air became shrouded and misty,
The bombers missed their target,
Cuthbert's miracle saved the city.

Tales by the score I could tell,
Of this saint, so faithful and true,
But go and kneel at the altar at Durham,
And you'll feel his presence touch you.

Many pilgrims travel to Durham,
To worship and adore at his shrine,
All colours, creeds and nationalities,
United as if by design.

Allied together we stand,
We plead – the – world – unanimous,
St. Cuthbert of Lindisfarne,
Pray for us.

## PILGRIMAGE TO HOLY ISLAND

I stepped from the mainland,
Into the crystal, clear sea,
Treading the water,
I felt god's hand on me.

It seemed that the missionaries,
And pilgrims of old,
Were walking with me,
Across the sand of gold.

I cherished their presence,
I lifted my face to see,
That St. Aidan was there,
And he was smiling on me.

I looked forwards and backwards,
And I was filled with awe,
To see the church crosses,
Stretching from shore to shore.

St. Bede and St. Cuthbert,
Told me to appreciate and write,
Of my feelings on viewing,
This wondrous, heavenly sight.

I sang as I walked,
I was trouble free,
As I trod the causeway,
I felt God's hand on me.

Honoured, loved and blessed,
I knew God was there,
I could not see Him,
But he stroked my hair.

Mary Nightingale Bell

All the Northern saints,
Looked down from above,
And they blessed this pilgrimage,
That told of our love.

That glorious, celestial day,
I felt privileged to be,
One of the pilgrims,
Who felt God's hand on me.

# AN EMBARRASSING INCIDENT

All dressed up
And nowhere to go
Oh – with me,
That is not so.

I'm going to the shops,
To get cake and bread,
Better write a note
Before it leaves my head.

Good morning Mrs. M.,
What a lovely day,
I greet lots of people
As I go on my way.

Everything seems normal,
Nothing out of place,
No startled expression
On anyone's face.

'Til I reach the bakers,
Standing in the queue,
I felt something snap,
What shall I do/

The assistant shouted,
Don't move, stand still,
It is me she meant,
O, to be invisible.

Mary Nightingale Bell

Slither – slither,
Plip, plip – plop,
I'm so embarrassed,
Will it never stop?

The queue then surrounded me
Looked at my feet,
Dare I look down
Go on have a peep.

I laughed with relief.
Have you guessed it girls,
The thing that snapped,
Was my imitation pearls.

## ALONE

Why did you leave me alone,
I didn't want to be on my own,
With no warning you went away,
I wanted you to stay,
But you left me, alone.

Why did we have to part,
You know you broke my heart,
You went without goodbye,
Didn't hear me cry,
Don't leave me alone.

I didn't know that day would be,
The worst in all the world to me,
You went, on your own,
And you should have known,
I'd be left, alone.

Amidst my fears,
I shed some tears,
And grieved for you,
Do you miss me too,
And watch me, all alone.

I walk the streets head held high,
I hope they didn't see me cry
For you, I miss you so,
Why did you have to go,
And leave me, all alone.

I had a walk along the sand,
I thought I felt you hold my hand,
We stood and gazed out at the sea,
I thought that you had come for me,
Because I was, alone.

Mary Nightingale Bell

Three sets of footprints there,
Whose was the extra pair?
Our Lord telling me he too,
Was concerned for me and you,
Because I was, alone.

I go to church and pray,
You'll come for me one day,
Never fear the Lord replied,
We'll always be by your side,
You'll never be, alone.

I go to church and kneel,
And as I do I feel,
You are with me again,
You are trying to make it plain,
I am not, alone.

As I walk down the aisle,
I look up at the altar and smile,
I have a secret I won't hide,
You and the Lord are by my side.
I am not, alone.

And in time at a future date,
We will meet at Heaven's Gate,
And then through eternity,
I will never be,
ALONE.

# BIG MEETING IN THE THIRTIES

Up at six in the mornin'
Catch the bus to Easington Lane,
Travel to our capital,
By puffing, spitting train.

Gannin' to Durham Big Meetin',
To get our pitmens rights,
Following our union banners,
Flying like bonny kites.

Putters, hewers, stonemen,
Brickies, datal hands,
United above the ground,
To the music of the colliery bands.

Black Prince and Hedley Hill,
Closed then I moved on,
In nineteen hundred and twenty eight,
To deep sea pit, Easington.

I look forward to this day,
To crack with my old marrers,
And we talk about the past,
And the future of our youngsters.

Unity and the future,
Slogans on front and back,
Pictures adorn our banners,
Fatalities draped in black.

Mary Nightingale Bell

Easington, Eppleton, Marsden,
Westoe, Haswell, Dawdon,
Murton, Blackhall, Vane Tempest,
Shotton, Thornley, Horden.

Marching from the station,
Bands playing for all they're worth,
To pitmen's families dancing,
My heritage - gold of the earth.

Stop at the County Hotel,
The band plays in a merry way,
To the balconies above,
Heavy with big names of the day.

Then, on to the racecourse,
Speeches in the afternoon,
Inspired, incited, heartened,
OUR DAY was over too soon.

# BEWITCHING NIGHT

One night a year,
I am allowed to roam,
To play ghostly tricks,
A warning – stay at home.

A weird apparition, lightning,
A vacuum in the sky,
It could be immaterial me,
As I flash fictitiously by.

My frenzied crazy laugh,
Will have you petrified screaming,
As I fly my magic broomstick
Tatty fluorescent hair streaming.

Do I mean you harm,
Is it all good fun,
Scared, uncertain, doubtful,
Then you'd better run.

A spectre might tug your hair,
A phantom pinch your cheek,
A shadow pop round the corner,
To play spooky hide and seek.

Beware to the courageously foolish,
Bewail the stupidly brave,
For on this unearthly night,
The sane go mad and rave.

Mary Nightingale Bell

Wailing, moaning, supernatural,
Mystical, genial, mean,
Hallucination, strange feelings,
Fear of seeing the unseen
Are unexplainable fancies,
You'll encounter on Hallowe'en.

# A LESSON OF LIFE

I learned my letters A to Zee,
I learned my lessons with zest,
My sums were never a problem to me,
At history I was one of the best.

I learned to tell the bad from the good,
To keep my temper in strife,
I was taught to behave how a lady should,
I thought I knew all about life.

I learned to cook ho a good wife aught,
I was blessed by the Lord above,
I got wed and then was taught,
Of a wonderful thing called love.

Sex, a new word I heard,
I thought it a what or a which,
The young ones said, How absurd,
Can't you tell a dog from a bitch.

I soon learned they didn't know much,
But I pondered how could I prove,
That I know all about sex and such.
But that doesn't equal love.

Sex and love, they've got it wrong,
They are two different lessons in life,
For true love as it says in the song,
Is special between husband and wife.

Mary Nightingale Bell

# ANTENATAL CHAT

It's your first,
I can always tell,
Morning sickness,
Not feeling too well,
Don't believe them,
It'll go away?
Got it for nine months,
I know what I say.

Was on the pill
When I first fell,
Bairn spit it out
With a triumphant yell.

Second, the coil,
With no time to spare,
Born in the ambulance,
Waving it in the air.

Third, the rhythm way,
Dates not my best thing,
She's a Go-Go dancer,
Result of a one night fling.

Condom, sheath
Were advised to me,
Who needs protection
From Aids or V.D.

Fingers tightly crossed,
Cap well in situ,
The fourth one arrived,
Right out of the blue.

## Where the Pits Were

Fallopian tubes tied,
Made these lot squirm,
Booking in again,
Blamed flying sperm.

Send him for the snip,
Which one would go?
I'm not married,
No time you know,
For wedding bells and rings,
Traditions, it's ironic,
Too busy attending,
The antenatal clinic.

Mary Nightingale Bell

# DERELICT HOUSE

Curtains flapping
from spaceless sockets
Staring from a house
that once had laughter
Parties and life
running through it.
Broken windows
door hanging off hinges
Rotten and broken gate
lying flat
In fly tipped yard
once swilled white.
Vibes of despair
poverty and gloom
Ooze from you
that once was home.
In Easington Colliery.
Look to the future,
bulldozers do your best
Leave a green field
as a memorial
To this house
It deserves no less.

# EASINGTON COLLIERY LOST

A disappearance,
It happened to me,
I am lost – I was
Easington Colliery.

Lost – no reward,
Not for me,
For I can never be found,
It is a mystery.

What happened to me,
People helped me grow,
I was a happy place,
Where did I go.

In 1910 people,
Flocked from all parts,
To form a community,
With honest, kind hearts.

Houses filled with life,
Happiness, work at the pit,
Vandalism and arson,
Sadly have come and changed it.

It was gradual,
The burden I had to bear,
People come here,
Throwouts of where?

It is like living,
Under a dismal cloud,
To see me dirty and dead,
Once I was so proud.

Mary Nightingale Bell

I am a dump,
Theft, drugs, alcohol are rife,
Move from here is the cry,
For a better life.

I am lost – no reward.
For I can never be found,
The pit is buried below,
I am destroyed above ground.

The words of this dirge,
Are so sad but true.

# SATISFACTION FROM CHANGES AT A HOSPITAL

I dance up the drive, I skip along,
The day is wonderful, I sing a song,
New life is coming, there'll be a birth,
A couple made happy, a new life on earth,
Will it be a girl or a baby boy,
Whichever it is it will bring great joy,
Go and phone home and tell everyone,]
And they'll all come and see the baby son.
Here's another young man, his heads in a whirl,
He's dancing with joy, he has a baby girl.
How wonderful every day was great,
It's changing now, I know the fate,
Of the hospital, the staff have been told,
It's a place for the dying and the old.
After the beginning we have an end,
Remember this as these patients we tend,
They were once someone's babies and then,
They grew to be girls and strong young men,
The years roll by they are old and grey,
They need our help when they get this way,
So I'll walk up the drive, head held high,
I'll sit at a bedside knowing someone will die,
I'll tend their needs, I'll hold their hand,
I'll comfort them from here to the promised land.
How can you do it, some people say,
See so much death every working day,
I do it with pride, I see at their end,
They are never lonely or afraid my friend,
And I thank God who put me on earth,
That I saw the miracle of a birth,
And then I learned the certainty of fate,
We all will come to heaven's gate.

Mary Nightingale Bell

No matter how or what we achieve,
Our years are numbered we have to leave,
Do not be troubled because we will see,
You leave this earth with dignity,
And as you die and slip away
You'll know I'll hold my rosary and pray,
That as I've tended you with love,
I'll know you are with the Lord above.

# SANTA CLAUS AND ME

I believe in Santa Claus,
I know some who do not,
Mrs. Grumpy said to me,
You know, it is all rot.

How can he climb upon your roof,
Slide down your sooty flue,
And leave great big parcels,
Under the tree for you.

She doesn't believe in Santa Claus,
Says it's in my silly mind,
But on Christmas morning,
I have presents of every kind.

I imagine Santa Claus,
Rides his sledge up in the air,
I never see him 'cept in my dreams,
But the presents are always there.

How do I get what I want,
Every single Christmas day?
I don't make a great big secret,
Of what I have to say.

When I shout up the chimney,
Or visit Santa in a store,
I make sure someone's listening,
To what I'm asking for.

They say that we must try,
To grant her wish because,
She's the only grown up that we know,
Who believes in Santa Claus.

Mary Nightingale Bell

Mrs. Grumpy says there is none,
So she can never receive,
Presents, gifts and surprises,
Because she doesn't believe.

So on a Christmas morning,
What has Mrs. Grumpy got,
No crackers, no nuts, no chocolate,
But I don't give a jot,
Because I believe in Santa Claus,
And I have got the lot.

# MIDNIGHT NEW YEARS EVE

The clock struck twelve,
The old year had gone,
Not moving an inch,
I was in the new one,
Five minutes ago,
I was wondering what to do,
To stay in the old,
Or go in to the new.

The clock struck twelve,
And before I knew it,
The New Years door opened,
And I was through it,
I'm wary of the new,
I like what I know,
But I had no choice,
I had to go.

The clock struck twelve,
I had forgotten,
You can't stay in the past,
You must go on.
I'm just human,
So I have no say,
I had to move on,
Into New Years Day.

Mary Nightingale Bell

The clock struck twelve,
Away with the old,
In the last few seconds,
I have grown bold,
The mystery of life,
Continues to baffle me,
Time won't stand still,
It's a challenge you see.

The old year is past,
Hurrah for the new,
Look forward to the unknown,
And Happy New Year to you.

# A CHILD IN WARTIME

In a cupboard,
Under the stairs,
Cushioned between
Mam and dad
I stand.

Noisy bombs
Snowing plaster
Thunderclaps clash
One minute panic
I fall.

Blue sky above
Eyes from dad's head
On the floor
Look at me
I scream.

A civilian orphan
An innocent
War taught me
To survive
I fight.

Mary Nightingale Bell

# SILENT MADNESS

Forbidden thoughts,
Crowd the head,
Confusion bounces,
Thoughts not said.

Swinging emotions,
Life's a seesaw,
Laugh and smile,
Then shout and roar.

Mind in a whirl,
Inside churns,
The seesaw levels,
Sanity returns.

## MY MOON

When I was a child,
The man in the moon,
Looked down and smiled,
With a round, kind face,
Made of cream cheese,
He chopped sticks and glowed,
I was safe and at ease,
When the full moon shone down on me.

In August, July and June,
Any month of the year,
I could rely on the moon,
To set romance astir,
Beaming a silvery dream path,
Rippling on sea to land,
As I strolled along the shore,
With my lover, hand in hand.

A crescent then a quarter,
Whole half, then full moon,
He'd watch, see and never tell,
Of how he cast a spell,
So that a special he,
Would think romantically,
And fall for my beguiling charms,
And long to hold me in his arms.

Then all my dreams were spoiled,
Human astronauts landed,
Walked on my moon's face,
As though an ordinary place,
Talked of dust, rocks and a crater,
My moon- computerised data,
No longer can lovers croon or spoon,
What have they done to my moon?

Mary Nightingale Bell

They think they've ruined my moon,
But we have an infinity,
From the midnight starry sky,
He looks down and winks his eye,
He shines down as he's always done,
So my lover and I still have fun,
From early July till Late June,
Under my magical, mysterious moon.

## THE PIT MANAGER'S HOUSE

I had this dream see,
Watching from the tree,
The carriage and pair,
Trot up
The tree lined,
Flower bordered drive.

Walking up the ten steps,
Between marble pillars,
Crinoline and top hat,
Proud as peacocks,
Going to tea,
In the pit managers' house.

Grandiose, Victorian mansion,
Statue on smooth lawns,
Flanked by an orchard,
Countless rooms and a hall,
Bathrooms, a library,
Multi windows, servants galore.

I had this dream see,
Watching from the tree,
Someday I'd have tea,
In the pit managers' house.

Nursing home for the aged,
Two hundred a week,
Tender loving care.
Time rolls on,
Great mansion gone.

Mary Nightingale Bell

Sitting in a room,
Against a wall lined with
Senile faces in chairs,
I cry at fate,
Who threw in my face,
My dream of having tea,
In the pit managers' house.

Alzheimer Annie,
Who's calling that name.
I have this dream see,
Sitting in a tree.

Look at the tears
Running down the grooves,
To her lips.
She's having tea
In the pit managers' house.

Me, I am in the tree,
Dreaming of having tea.

# GEORGE AND PAPERMOON

Faithful man and his dog,
Dressed for the moody weather,
Steps paced and measured,
As one, moving together.

Fog, sun, cutting wind,
Rain or blinding snow,
Better to bracingly stride the land,
Than toil in danger below.

Steadily walking unclocked miles,
For love of contest and race,
Pleasure and pride in his hobby,
Expression contentment of face.

Sleek, slim, groomed,
Hallmark of a pedigree,
Strict diet and exercise,
Perfection twinned suitably.

Devotion in the tone of his voice,
Can be felt in the tender sound,
Partnered show respect and regard,
Of the pitman for his racing greyhound.

Mary Nightingale Bell

# I WAS A WITNESS

That young man,
Looks shifty to me,
Is he casing the joint,
To do a robbery?

I have watched him,
Pace up and down,
Looking very guilty,
His hat pulled well down.

He glances up the street,
Sees no one around,
Dashes into the shop,
With - one bound.

I open the door,
He's run up the stairs,
I'll follow him,
Catch him unawares.

I pause at the top,
Watch from the landing,
I see the young man,
He's sitting not standing!

This chair he's sat in,
Frightened to be seen on,
Guess – where-it is,
A ladies beauty salon.

I looked in amazement,
I laughed till I cried,
That macho young man,
Was having his eyelashes dyed.

## MINER NOT REINSTATED

Did any miner think,
As he stood on the picket line,
That fighting to keep the pits open,
He'd be banned from every mine.

Down the perilous pit,
Warned by his Davey lamp,
Lurked an invisible enemy,
Methane gas, unseen firedamp.

But on riding to bank,
He thought everyone a marra,
Then in the strike of eighty four,
He found himself in a dilemma.

As warrior like he stood,
Shouted and bellowed,
From a secret hiding place,
Unseen he was being videoed.

What were his puzzled thoughts,
As he was arrested from the crowd,
Why should he be punished,
For speaking his thoughts aloud.

Sirens screaming, blue lights flashing,
He was taken to a cell,
Treat like a notorious criminal,
For serving his union well.

Now he sits and ponders,
And he will his whole life long,
What historians will debate in the future,
Was he right or wrong.

Mary Nightingale Bell

# I HATE WOMEN'S LIB

I loved the olden days,
I loved the young men's ways,
They looked at women with awe,
Stopped and opened every door,
Want a seat- pulled out a chair,
A job to do- they were there,
After you, my dear they said,
If ever they were a step ahead,
Never heard them curse and swear,
Called me madam and old men sir,
Things changed, what went wrong,
Some younger women came along,
They wanted equality with man,
Thought it was a wonderful plan,
Same pay, same work etc. dears,
They've spoilt the pleasure of years and years,
For a couple of pounds what have we got,
Think very carefully not a lot,
Do it yourself, don't ask them,
They must be laughing these young men,
Halve the bill when you go out for a meal,
Who was it wanted this deal,
Young women, dense, naïve and dim,
We through the ages had ruled over him,
Who thought that he, was head of the house,
We pretended to be like a timid mouse,
But we always got our own way,
Were cosseted, loved and spoiled every day,
You young women ruined a good life,
When you got equality for a wife.

## ON THE WAY TO CHURCH

Sunday mornings,
Give me a devilish feeling,
The street to myself,
Offbeat imagination reeling.

Hop, skip and jump twice,
Handstand against a door,
I perform these athletic acts,
Then go on to do more.

Balancing on the car park wall,
I cartwheel, legs waving,
Upright I jump on and off,
A gymnast satisfying a craving.

Bound on to the bus shelter top,
Render the Indian Love call,
My pseudo soprano echoing,
As if in the great Albert hall.

Tap dance, then a quick twirl,
Like Gene Kelly in the rain,
Twisting, rocking and singing,
To a heavy rock metal refrain.

I am nearly at the church,
Tidy clothes, that are akimbo,
Comb hair, straighten face,
Check reflection in a shop window.

Stride with confidence, head held high,
To the middle of the empty street,
Bowing to my unseen audience to hear,
Encores for my mad cap feat.

Mary Nightingale Bell

Turn round, oh my what's this,
Cricket eleven as a matter of fact,
Waiting for the league mini bus,
Have they witnessed my bizarre act?

Exchange greetings and smiles,
No sign of stunned fascination,
Alas this exclusive performance,
Is in my reeling imagination.

# PASSING THROUGH

I was born long ago,
With an ambition to do,
Something to be remembered for,
As I was passing through.

I enjoyed most of life,
Grew older and wise too,
And I felt I must make a mark,
As I was passing through.

I prayed to God,
Give me something to do,
He said – rhyme everything
As you are passing through.

A century from now,
Will they ask who,
Was the Mary Bell who wrote,
As she was passing through.

A blessing and a gift,
Granted to a few,
You'll see I rhymed everything,
As I was passing through.


I'm inspired by life,
The old and the new,
And I wrote of loved ones,
As I was passing through.

Mary Nightingale Bell

Read through my works,
Who inspired me most,
'Twas the people of England,
On the North East coast.

I loved them all,
Yes, everyone of you,
Hope you remember me,
After I have passed through.

# TARTARUS

Colours – the artist in me jumped
At the strange macabre scene,
Dazzling, shooting fast forward,
Orange, red, blue, brown, green.

That ochre face, is, it a real thing,
No eyes in its blank, mauve sockets,
A giant hand carefully carved,
Adding a necklace of golden lockets.

Each showing their own picture,
Of a strange, barbaric being,
Still as statues in stone,
Inactive, dormant, overseeing.

An angel or a devil,
Beckoning arms outstretched,
An evil grin, pitying smile,
Puzzled I cried out and retched.

Footprints climb up the sheer wall,
A monument sprouts from the sea,
A mystical pipe, a romantic bridge,
Smooth stones, monstrous eggs, fantasy.

A passage, a cave with no ceiling,
The floor a bottomless pit,
A freak of nature watching,
Crouched dinosaur, apocalit.

A landslide, a volcanic eruption,
Piles of rubble, stones and slate,
Pit waste, unwanted machinery,
It depends how you look and translate.

## Mary Nightingale Bell

Man versus the mysteries of Nature,
Machine versus rain, wind and sun,
A battle of immovable wills,
Immortal Nature easily won.

Is this place in Outer Space.
No it's within easy reach,
A weird dream, a scary nightmare,
It is Easington Colliery beach.

# MOURNING

In the madding crowd,
I glimpsed your face,
Called your name,
You did not turn,
Followed you,
All in vain,
I was left,
With loneliness.

You stroked my hair,
We made some plans,
Laughed and loved,
Then I awoke,
Beyond belief,
It was a dream,
I was left,
With loneliness.

I have a friend,
He holds my hand,
I try to think,
That he is you,
Despairing,
Is there no escape,
Or freedom,
From loneliness.

Good friends advise,
Cast off your black,
Mourning's over,
No cure for me,
Only half,
Of what I used to be,
Surrounded,
By loneliness.

## Mary Nightingale Bell

I am brave,
I brainwash me,
Into believing,
I've come to terms,
With what had to be,
I try to cope,
Without you,
And loneliness.

# MARY NIGHTINGALE BELL

Mary Nightingale Bell nee Duff was born in Easington Colliery in 1930, attended Easington Colliery Infants and Junior Schools and then Seaham Harbour Girls Grammar School. After marrying and three children later she became a nurse and what else with a name like Nightingale. Mary has had many stories and poems published and is currently working on a book about life in Easington Colliery in the twentieth century.

Printed in Great Britain
by Amazon.co.uk, Ltd.,
Marston Gate.